Between the Pillars

Between the Pillars

Poems by

Hannah Darling Fenn

Cover design by Shay Culligan
Cover image by William Morris
Author photo by Matthew Billingsley

ISBN: 978-1-63980-649-2

Kelsay Books
502 South 1040 East, A-119
American Fork, Utah 84003
Kelsaybooks.com

For my father, John E. Darling

Acknowledgments

Thank you to the following publications, in which versions of these poems previously appeared:

Cordella Magazine: "Pillars," "Tendering"
fsm. Arts Journal: "The Bluff to Which We Sang"
Terrible Orange Review: "Helix," "And Such"
Wilde Magazine: "When the Art Is Subtle"

Contents

The Bluff to Which We Sang

The ancient future holds us dear
In its little itinerary.
It hums along our hay fire,
Singing rain, please breathe
With us.

It's my favorite ghost story.
The way the land hasn't given us
Signal to leave.
And we start to become the plains
And he starts to wear work boots.
And I wonder if everything has crawled
Its way home at some point and felt
The forgiving earth soften under elbows.

And Such

This is a night desert walk
And her second rebirth
Has gone a bit tipsy turvy.

Which feels like peace washed over.
Which feels like a highway chant coming home.
Which is not of the flesh.

But made in her ethereal house
Where wayfaring crows hold up
Each picket of fence
And wide circles of the by and by
Split like some broken ring of earth
And ache for her to sing them whole.

Her son has this face
Which harbors some engulfed vibration
Of every forest she walked
Before him.
And another wild-less howl:
Let your babies . . .
Cowboys.

Tendering

Sometimes at night,
She takes off her magnolia mask—
Which is hot with fever—
Places it on the armchair,

And ignites it.
And the hours open then
Like little weightless doors.

And it's eighty degrees at 1 a.m.
Which is so docile and time-brewed
That she slides nicely from
Mindset to mindset.

And the roughening of every
Driftless barn animal claws its way into
The belly of things.

And the belly of things
Was us!
All along.
It was us.

But you'd rather read that book
Than shout about it.
You'd rather sing this heart home.
And then you see
Her somber mouth is just the lay of the land.

Helix

There was an orb signaled
And a mother soaking her hair in coffee
With shoes kicked off
And no showmanship to the ether.

And I found the center of all my lives
On a hot summer sidewalk at dusk.
With the crickets and thick melting
Nostalgia.

And a thousand denim babies
Asking me when we're going to the store.

When will we buy ourselves.
When will we rest on her earth.
When will we sip cold soda like children
And build the long ladders

Like a helix
That have us at the bottom
And us at the top.

At the Drive-Thru

"What do you want?" is too
Depth-y a question for those
About to depart.
But if I had to choose something,
I'd say the glow of the menu
Showing me your hands
And the hum of the engine
Lacing our lighter
Selves into the night.

Dove's Mighty Crossing

The mighty roads taken,
They're of little earthly good.
Like myths falling.

We veer with your silent language instead.

The celestial whims
Have gotten us much farther.

And here we've seen the gods on break,
Shifting the landscape of a place
Just by being there.

Like you and I do.

Playing cards and braiding grass
And breathing in all the thoughts ever thought
And making a simple clay bowl from them,

Just on a whim.

When the Art Is Subtle

It looked like an iridescent soak,
The living room.
And the way this hot spring of the life
We've chosen opened between us.

I tell you I only feel at home
When the message is indirect.

That's how I felt then.
When we read the script we typed.

And it was like the only towels
We had were made of things
That shouldn't be in the house—
Daisy weeds,
Fresh dew,
Receipts for dead solar star infused soil.

We have the only wild lawn
In the neighborhood.
It's okay,
I like being wrapped
In the earth anyway, you said.

And we moved to the unkempt backyard
With our broken watches and drank coffee
In the lawn chairs and wore straw hats
That gave us new, quiet ideas
Like, *just sit by the fire.*

Limbless as We Are

The unlost lover
Of a cliff's edge
Knows no difference between
Broken heat and what was never said.

He sometimes reaches for fire,
It sometimes reaches him.

But if grounding meant
Lawfulness,
He would always choose
The way of flight in limbs.

Nobility of Palms, Proceed to the Route

Both harness and let your wolves run
In the bilateral crossing of calcified forest.
A place we go for cloudy tea.
A place we saw a saint cry for her boy,
As he hammered out the walls
Of a garage in soft blasts
And we learned what non-permanence meant.

Pillars

And on the blooming hill
She pats my hair dry with a towel.
Comes rung of wash and sinew;
Dislodging my stacked dreamhood.

Milk-haired midwestern mothers line the corridors
And tell me I'm delicate in that forlorn way.

And I sit between the pillars.
Clay in my hands, hum in my mouth.
Knowing light is what falls between them.
Knowing neutrality in the way of astral time.

The Starve

When willed and blind
A source does come
To sink me to the hearth.

And nothing does a tortured
Dance like me to it
Unbirthed.

These aching palms
Do like to meet
And ask which waters
Do you look on?

Are these them?
These burning ones?
The same ones that I drink from?

It was then we saw
We weren't the ones
But standing near transpired.

A blooming scape,
A giving well,
To none ourselves the liars.

We needed most to ring that bell
To know it wasn't fire.

But that unmet hunger,
That empty dose,
Yes, it was that feeding
Which truly fed us both.

The Gods of High-Hanging Clotheslines

Two clotheslines hung in town,
High, high above the dry grass fields.

And the longest white sheets ever sewn
Billowed around this most quiet day.

This is a wide-open space
And there aren't many thoughts or have-to's.

The people just embody this having of a body,
Much like gentle animals.

Understand: this is a small town
That might've existed somewhere like Nebraska.

And some wear a crown yet sit on the earth
When the wind is strong.

They see printing on the sheets, reading things like:
The in between is heavenly.

You are composite angels, but don't know it
And when betrothed to the unseen,
You may feel a bit lost.

But wear
Tight the ring.

These quiet people gather 'round
To drum beneath the ancient writing.

And it pleases them.
And the fertile ground
And the gods of high-
Hanging clotheslines too.

Fortune Teller

A stingray formed itself for me,
Into an orb,
At the shoreline of iridescence,

And mentioned
How I didn't wear sandals that day.

I knelt by him.
He dispelled my future past
From sand to water and
In his glow he said,

There wouldn't be a sunset this
Evening, for the sky became
A fabric.

An accidental dial.

Going.
Going.
Gone.

Lake Michigan

I'm on one side of her.
And on the other,
is where my father grew up.

I sometimes feel the current
Bringing me his words.
In some lapse of space and time.

But we forgot the beach towels again.

Searching Intuit Online

They would confidently intuit
Your very thoughts.
I can intuit.
I can *almost* feel.
However, surged, with additional
Meanings.

It's like:
Different ways to say January 25.

He intuited the old sayings and his
Consciousness.
It was a rational
Process, hiding information.
It was universal!
Beware of this.

Don't tell me
That words are out of bounds.
I get lost.

Stay-at-home moms should be
Able to intuit when a child is ill.
And the judge has not yet issued
His opinion explaining this one.

We cannot find it exhaustive.
You have truth values,
But I only trust the stars.

Of Book Spines

The afterlife and the gifts of unknown things
Are sometimes a great notion.
Play the quiet game and
Follow the constellations home.

The testimony and the balcony are
Sacred mirrors, dream dials, a book of hours.
I never promised you a rose garden,
I am just the man
Who walked through time.

Sun God in Midsummer

The sun god walks to the theater in the afternoon.
(Luminaries need leisure too).

Her dress is white and long in summer
And she goes barefoot.

She finds large poems laid in the woods
And she reads them.

Then reads the playbill
And adores the mountains.

The actors are joyful,
Which pleases her,
For she knows the day is
Eternal.

Call Ourselves Poets

If we're really going to call
Ourselves poets, then maybe
We'll eat breakfast on the porch.

And we'll see in laundry piles
On the couch, all the smallest
Villages and we'll imagine
Their clay outposts overlooking
Cliffs where maybe the leaders
Have a quiet meeting about
The possibility of war or peace.

And the grapefruit we ate
On the porch is all
Sun sinew with traces of some
Life cycle, like fruit
That was designed perfectly
For delicate humans.

Ah so, some mantra
To erase time.

The Mare

Let's meet the people
At the Pillars of Hercules.

In the marshes, the mare
Shakes her hooves,
Latent powers and divine static
Laying fresh in spring air.

The son of Mars intends with quiet
Ears to please the gods and really,
Mark off the to-do list.

He will fall, but he knows how to.
He has put the basic impulse of budding life
In some plane of mind for us.

And we keep it in small pouches on our belts,
Sowing it dearly in fields
To reap the world anew.

Muse/Earth

We stir the visible from the unseen
In crafts of hand and mind,
Like a prayer where the land
Meets our lake's edge—
Don't dismiss us.

Let us know a peek
Of your magic that we
Might transcribe it
Before our return home.

Quiet Fire

I've dripped wax on the stairs
Moving through our winter things
And tossing old shrugs around.

The kids tear at it and ask why some things
Stain and some don't.

I've never known how to write, really.
But it howls me down and offers unrest
In its absence.

Sometimes the map is blurred
And we build this old sort of nest
On the living room floor
And you say
Well, the birds
Are taken care of and so are we.

And I mean, our bodies are of the same.
Just wax forming and unforming.

//

I was walking through the mall—
Even the plastics and neon lights
Did not tire me—
Just more stuff of the ether.

And they told me:
We miss you while you're on earth,
just as much as you miss us.

31

Water Which Does Not Wet the Hands

There is the never-touched, which remembers
Deep in the clay,

Which I know is you.

There is the shadow slowly watching its
Object.

There is dawn: the gate of some temple,
Undescribed, but familiar to all.

There is the water which does not wet the hands.

There is the being that carries our home to us
Over many miles.

There is a subtle heaven in pouring for the son,

There is a falling, where my knees are the ground
And the ground is your knees.

There is a day held in the unopened eyes.

Which, still, I know is you.

Be Here Now, I Suppose

A quiet chanting comes
From the grandmother in
The house across the street
While we unload
The groceries from the car.

It's soothing and out of place.
It's the sudden
Re-enchantment of daily living.

And right now, I don't have ears that can
Hear what you're telling me about a
Lost bag of oranges
or a major lapse in time,

While she lights these little candles
In the windowsill and hums
The heavens right down into
Our driveway.

About the Author

Hannah Darling Fenn is a poet and artist from Ashland, Oregon, where she resides with her husband and three children. She's a freelance writer, as well as co-founder and co-editor of Gossamer Arts, a literary magazine. Hannah holds a bachelor's degree in English with a minor in creative writing from Southern Oregon University. She feels most at home in the mountains with her sons or dreaming up worlds and writing poems in coffee shops. She is a third generation published author.

www.ingramcontent.com/pod-product-compliance
Lightning Source LLC
Chambersburg PA
CBHW031009090426

42737CB00008B/746